Avalon Breen

Dismantled

A Collection

of Poetry and Prose

Avalon Breen

Avalon Breen

Cover art and illustrations by Zachary Hampson

Edited by Katie Carlin

Proofread by Joanne Sexton

"Avalon Breen's debut collection of poetry and prose 'Dismantled' provides a memorising insight into the complications of venomous relationships, facades, sense of self and self-actuality. An impressive debut collection, Breen's experience with a previous partner's flirtation, often mistaken as devotion, inspired her writing. Her aim is to help the reader through their own process of healing. Breen's artistry and relatability in her work provides this path for the reader. She uses language to combat the acts of an ex-lover. Her words transform into monuments that many can find comfort in. this collection showcases how the darkest, bruising and disillusioned loves can develop into tender self-expressionistic words of art. Breen's collection of poetry and prose has the power to speak to any individual who has been through love or needs comfort in embracing the journey of healing. Not only does the collection reflect on the destructive and loud aspects on the relationship, it dives into the intricate, silent moments that occur behind closed doors. It is for the heart-broken and the heart-breaker. The collection reflects one yet thousands of individual's experiences with intimacy and heartbreak. "Dismantled" demonstrates how fragmenting and cursing love can be in a thought-provoking way that inspires the readers to find wholeness again.

The collection is similar to the work of Edgar Holmes 'Her Favourite Color Was Yellow' through its minimalistic design and use of line illustrations. The short poems and prose capture the complexity of heartache beautifully. Breen finds her internal forms of fulfilment as she journeys through control, fleeing, breaking, releasing and strengthening. Her collection is timeless, speaking to individuals of the past, present and future worldwide. This collection is not simply for the modern millennial female; it has the command to transform the minds of any individual"

Katie Livermore, Teacher

"So many individuals have been through breakups, toxic or not but it's strange how the feelings we feel are rarely talked about. Reading the poems in this book is like talking to a friend who is giving you honest advice. It's a book I wish I had read when I was going through a dark time, but reading it now, I am truly inspired by her healing. Avalon writes purely from her heart and openly shares her raw emotions. Sometimes the ideology of love is so warped and sugar-coated; but reading Avalon's words gives the reader such an open and honest representation on how relationships can be. The feelings you feel after a breakup are complex and not spoken about enough; often we bottle them up and allow them to tear us apart from the inside out. Reading this honestly was like a breath of fresh air because it's nice knowing that others are feeling the same way too; it's okay to feel the way we feel. The promotion of self-love and the importance of healing that Avalon writes about within her book are words that I truly believe can inspire and help others who are on or have been on a similar journey. From beginning to end I was hooked on Avalon's story, and I was surprised by how relatable each poem was to my own. The way she writes is so personable and no matter who you are, I can guarantee you will gain something from Avalon's poetry. Seeing the gradual shift from negativity to positivity within her book not only allows the reader to follow Avalon on a path of heartbreak and recovery, but also the transformation is also incredibly inspiring"

Laura Tedder, Artist

"Avalon courageously gives voice to terrain of the heart that is so often silenced in her first literary offering *Dismantled*. She eloquently brings forth that which is broken, deluded, scarred, and fragmented. Through vignettes or snapshots of her past relationship, we see all the colours and shade of brokenness laid bare. As readers and human beings, we know this landscape though we rarely speak of it, even to ourselves. Avalon's genius lies in giving these feelings a unique shape that, at the same time, resonates universally. These glimpses strike a chord with the dark parts of our hearts. In this way Avalon's words are deeply acknowledging, allowing us space and time to reflect on heartbreak and the decimation we have all felt through losing parts of ourselves in love.

In the second part of her book 'Wholeness' Avalon expresses her insight into the journey of healing and recovery. The ultimate revelation that the love we so often seek from external sources, can only ever be found within, is reinforced throughout. With honesty, wisdom and tender insight Avalon invites us into a more loving and compassionate relationship with ourselves. *Dismantled* is a raw and evocative work which promises to be a guiding and gentle presence for anyone healing from the depths of brokenness. This is a real gift and one I am grateful to Avalon for having the courage to share with the world."

Elizabeth Mcarthy, Author of "The Art of Self-Compassion"

Avalon Breen

Preface

The inspiration for this book was born of my own personal journey of healing, one that came after spending years in a toxic relationship. It was truly a relationship in which we brought out the worst in each other. Possession, control, emotional blackmail, manipulation, guilt, self-indulgence, ego, and suffocation pervaded those years of my life. On the surface, everything appeared fine, but behind the façade, I'd wake up every day feeling heavier and go to bed feeling something deeper than exhaustion, and more damaging than just depletion.

Returning to myself after such a relationship was laced with deep emotional difficulty. The price tag for the strength I now have was the pain I endured back then. These poems, which I began six years ago, have now found physical form in the pages of this book. However, despite being written by me, this book is not intended for me. The true objective of this work is to help you, the person reading these words, through your own process of healing. My story is merely the beginning of this project; it has since taken on a life of its own. I pray that you find value in my words that is unique to you and your life.

Avalon Breen

Avalon Breen

Fragmented

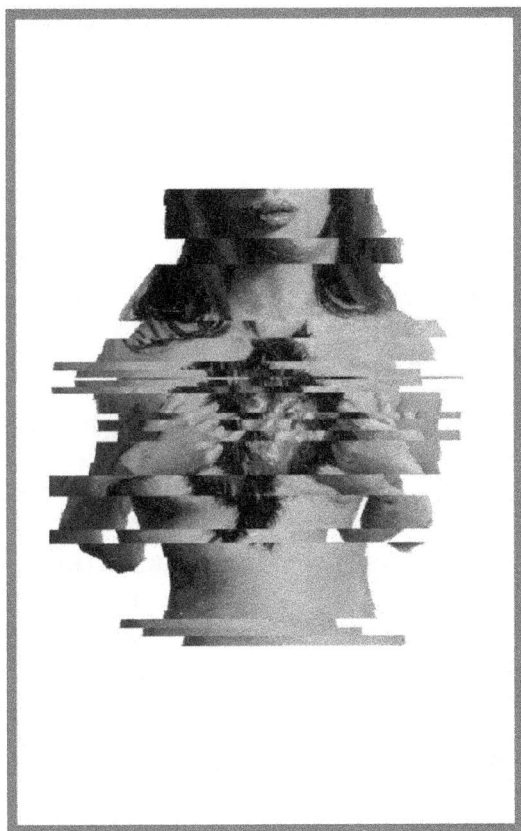

To be fragmented connotes the process of breaking or shattering into pieces. When in the midst of heartbreak, an unfortunate condition of both love and life, the word "fragmented" dissolves from being a hollow language device and melts into an essence of greater meaning, one that encapsulates the embodiment of the brokenness we feel.

The heights of love can be so intoxicating; the ecstasy, the euphoria, and the honey-soaked elation. The fall from such a height is like being pushed off a skyscraper. Sudden, sharp, and overwhelming, with a devouring sense of shock and disbelief. An onslaught of questions invades our minds. Encased within the turbulence of our thoughts, we are then hit by the all-consuming pain of plummeting to the ground. How will we view love after this? What emotions will arise when we think of loving again? How can we ever imagine braving those heights again after barely surviving our last fall? Will we turn our hurt into anger, resenting the mountaintop of love? Or will we never climb again, knowing that we are safest closer to the ground?

The ways in which we deal with heartache are subjective, yet we all experience it at some point in our lives. The saying "love is blind" describes perfectly our state when deep in love- the rest of the world becomes a blur as our vision is fixated on the best side of our lover and is blinkered to their flaws. We are lost, happily, within another world, one that seems exclusive to us and our lover. When this powerful force abandons us and our hearts are left broken, the remnants of that love is transformed, mutated. We're left with feelings of anguish, powerlessness, pain, sorrow, melancholy, and regret.

The first section of this book is concerned with such emotions; however, the nuances of love and heartbreak can never be entirely conveyed within the limitations of these linguistic confines. Throughout the book, my words touch on other feelings, such as infatuation, lust, attachment, or obsession. Hearts break for many different reasons, in many different ways; there is heartbreak of falling out of love, or a love that remains unrequited, or perhaps you've known a "love" that has hurt you, forgotten you, mislead you or even abused you. The scope of emotions that are born from such an experience cannot be narrowed down or labelled, no matter how hard we may try. It is rather my aim to reflect the many shades of brokenness that can come from love, no matter how ineffable a task this may be. My earnest wish is that these words serve you. Allow them to bring you comfort in your darkest moments of despair and despondency; we all feel pain; we just express it in different ways. Love and heartbreak turn everyone's world upside-down. May this book help you realise you are not alone in what you're feeling.

Most of all, whatever stage of life or love you are in, honour your feelings. Embrace them. Give them space to breathe. To exist. Don't shut them down or repress them. I assure you, if you do, they will manifest in much uglier, darker ways later on. Healing is a process and the first step requires you to feel whichever emotions you have – not deny them. You don't need to act out on them; just allow them to be.

Let these words be your companion on your journey. I hope they help to awaken the strength in you to heal yourself.

Avalon Breen

Temporal

We failed right from the start.

We were searching for something infinite

When this was only ever transient.

Tapestry

Your words have woven stories into the tapestry of my body
that no one will ever be able to unthread.

Avalon Breen

Silence

So many things you wanted to say, but you just let the silence
speak for you.

Avalon Breen

Foundations

I write this for you.

Every syllable.

Every letter.

Everything that I do.

Like a bridge to your heart,

I lay down my ink like bricks,

Hoping that these linguistic constructions

Can build our love anew.

Avalon Breen

Dark Knight

You had my heart

So I adorned you with love

And affection,

Then, to my very own dejection,

Discovered I was only part

Of a collection,

Another nameless victim

To a connoisseur of hearts

And master of such a dark

Art.

Avalon Breen

Catastrophe

You and me,

Oh, what a beautiful catastrophe.

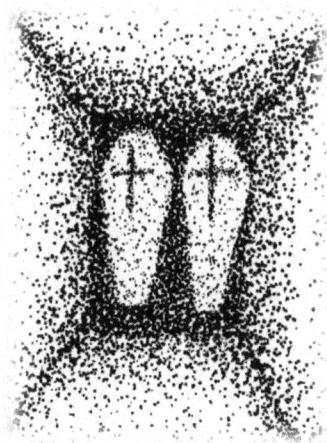

Silly Girl

I only wanted to be warmed by your love.

How silly of me to think that I was impervious to being burned.

Old Chapter

I'm trying to rewrite my story but how can I when you've always been the one holding the pen?

Avalon Breen

Timeless Eulogies

Haven't you realised it yet?

My poems are eulogies for our deceased love.

Avalon Breen

Masterpiece

He is the artist that painted me in his colours, now my breaths
are just hues of him.

Delicate

You mustn't disturb the repose of such a fragile rose. Her petals are withering from being overexposed.

So I've encased her within this tender prose. Where she will rest within poetry's fragrant meadows.

Freeze-frame

I live between these lines.

Breathing in vowels and exhaling consonants.

Bending to the will of their narrow confines.

Hoping to transform words into monuments.

And crystallise that time when you were mine.

Avalon Breen

Deaf Ears

Sometimes, I am unsure what is more deafening;

The words you speak or the ones you don't.

Avalon Breen

Untouchable

You remind me of water,

Sometimes so vast and impenetrable,

So expansive that every day, I discovered a new ocean hidden
within you.

Other times, you were soft and untouchable,

I could feel you slip between my fingers as I tried to hold you
within my palms

Only for you to dissolve out of my grasp.

Embers

I was always your wax stick on this candle.

Holding you up,

Giving you a place to live,

Risking my own existence,

Knowing I would be burned and reduced to ashes,

All of this just to indulge in the warmth of but a fleeting flame.

Avalon Breen

Ocean Floor

Your love is a raging ocean

That pulls me from the shore

As you ebb and flow like a heartbeat;

I am immersed within your depths.

Yet when storms come

And the tide is stronger

And I begin to drown

You leave me gasping for air.

Avalon Breen

The Fate of the Wilting

Poor flower, drooping with regret

Over things she wishes she could forget,

Yet memories have far too many silhouettes;

If only you and I had never met.

Love always did have the heaviest of debts.

I guess heartbreak is forever beset,

Is this the fate of just another Juliet?

Outweighed

How silly of me to realise this was nothing more than a
dalliance,

bewitching souls and seducing hearts must be just some of your
many talents,

for the scales of love are very rarely ever balanced;

besides, who could ever win against the weight of such malice?

Avalon Breen

Illusion

What a devastating thing it is,

placing me upon this pedestal,

crowning me your queen;

a distorted muse.

What an ostentatious show,

a flawless façade,

an impenetrable pretence,

built upon abuse.

If only they knew

the secrets kept behind closed doors

yet the key hides within that devilish grin,

the one that has them all so enthused.

Brokenness is never visible

to those not looking beyond the surface;

what a tragedy it is,

to believe this heart can be reused.

Avalon Breen

Untouchable

Your memory is always visiting,

despite my attempts at distancing,

your image is never dwindling,

instead it is forever glistening,

because I won't ever stop envisioning,

even though my sanity you are inhibiting,

yet I am failing at my attempts of extinguishing,

your love is something I won't ever be relinquishing.

Nature of the Ego

Too afraid and egos too inflated to admit that we care.

So we try to show each other in convoluted ways how we feel
but never say it out loud.

We wouldn't even dare.

I know the day is approaching when we will grow sick of this
game but still lack the courage to say what we feel, what we've
always felt.

So I'll settle for the next lover and you'll take on a wife.

We'll both go our separate ways and live our lives.

Always to be haunted by the death of three words that never got
the chance to be voiced.

Impermanent

Our love was only ever a type of evanescence;

Conceived in impermanency, we were never meant to last,

But even so, what a beautiful decadence.

I guess time just held us too tightly in her grasp.

Avalon Breen

Façade

We disguised the word attachment and passed it off as love. The camouflage worked seamlessly until suddenly we were standing in the wake of our shattered pretence. Stunned at our wasted effort and empty hearts.

Avalon Breen

Fragility

It's such a fragile thing, to exist in your memories.

You forget while I fade.

Avalon Breen

Hand Prints

My body still aches from the fingerprints you left behind.

How am I expected to erase the memory of your breath
entwined with mine?

Each mark a tangible reminder of the imprint you've given me,

I thought that the love we shared would transcend eternity.

Avalon Breen

A Mouthful

The flavour of your skin still lingers upon my lips.

I wonder how deep beneath it am I still.

Thoughtless

I should have known from your generic script

That your intentions weren't hard to decrypt.

Avalon Breen

Memories of the Heart

Can you still feel my presence?

Or is it lost within memory's purgatory?

Surely a heart cannot forget a lover's essence.

Pain

It's a feeling that I cannot describe.

I never thought it would affect me so.

I always knew you'd move on, and I thought I had too.

So why is the image of her and you

Evoking feelings that I can't subdue?

Heartache

Whenever I spoke to you, you shut your ears,

Whenever I tried to look you in the eyes, you closed them.

Whenever I went to take your hand in mine, you clenched your fingers,

Whenever I leaned in to kiss you, your lips were sealed together.

And when I tried to love you, you shielded your heart.

The Fate of Poets

I don't know whether I should be thanking you.

truth be told you've given me something to express.

but I still don't know if that makes me more fortunate or
unfortunate.

you see, the thing is, when it comes to heartbreak, everyone's
cursed to feel it.

I just happen to be cursed to write about it as well.

Avalon Breen

Bleeding Love

You swallow roses and bleed thorns

For a love you're destined to mourn.

Avalon Breen

Elusive

I'm paralysed between the moments we had and the ones that always eluded us.

Delectable

I remember watching the sweetness drip from your lips when you would talk to me in love letters. I remember the goose-bump riddled skin, and laughter in love-soaked air. I remember kisses that had no curfew and caresses softer than clouds.

Oh, how a love so sweet has a most bitter aftertaste...

Avalon Breen

Unforgettable

It is haunting, the way you linger.

How your fingerprints persist on my skin

Long after you are gone.

In the corner of my eye, I see your figure

Or perhaps a shadowy apparition of what's passed.

My mind is quite the trickster.

The memories, they plague me.

Your voice torments my ears relentlessly.

Is this the curse I must bear for once being your sinner?

Avalon Breen

Fleeting

I used to sip on your words like a sweetness untasted,

Relishing in the flavour of your voice and its softness as it would gently brush my ears.

You were a delicacy that can only ever be sampled.

And now I'm ready to be dismantled.

Explain to Me

Tell me how touches so sweet and love so tender fades.

Tell me how promises are turned to dust and vows become empty sounds.

Tell me how late-night discourses and endless embraces are reduced to blurred memories.

Tell me, how it is that people fall out of love?

Avalon Breen

Antithesis of Love

We never really knew how to love each other. All we knew was how to escape the gnawing loneliness by immersing ourselves in each other. A shallow deception on both our parts.

Avalon Breen

Irony

Ironic, isn't it? Here I was, hoping you'd bring me salvation. But a person like you could only ever bring damnation.

Avalon Breen

Running After You

I'm running out of things to think. Things to say. Things to write. Things to do. So I'm running away from running now. Because I realise that you were never chasing me anyway.

Avalon Breen

Right at the Wrong Thing

Our story was filled

with so many successful

goodbyes that really

were all our failed

don't go's.

Avalon Breen

Delusion

I thought you were the shield that protected me.

The house that sheltered me.

The impenetrable presence I always felt around me.

But all these things did was collapse in on me

and now I'm buried under the weight of you.

Avalon Breen

Curiosity

I wonder if you guys talk about me when you're together. Do I ever come up in conversation? If so, when? Is it in your usual exchanges? Is it when you're arguing? I wonder what you say about me to her. Does my name dart out of her mouth like a bullet to your chest? Or does it fall gently off your tongue like a frequent visitor?

Avalon Breen

Retrospect

Looking back, I realise you were just some honey-flavoured poison.

Avalon Breen

Empty

Without your voice, even the noise seems so silent.

Without your smile, even the sun seems so dim.

Without your presence, even the dawn seems so colourless.

Without your love, everything seems like nothing.

Avalon Breen

You vs Me

You laugh while I lament.

You smile while I suffer.

You glorify while I grieve

You enjoy while I endure.

You forget while I fade...

Avalon Breen

Temptation

You were a forbidden fruit

I couldn't wait to taste,

A rare sweetness I could

Never hope to waste.

Your flavour made more than

Just my heart race,

But now you're just another

Mouthful I'm trying to erase.

Avalon Breen

Reversing Time

I often press repeat and rewind

On our forgotten tune,

Savouring the aroma of another time,

the moments shared last June,

the days when I was yours and you were mine,

I see now that when it comes to heartbreak, no one is immune.

Avalon Breen

The Depths

I was drowning you

You were drowning me

Maybe we're both too good at subtly.

Avalon Breen

Residue

My words no longer feel my own.

They feel like the empty remnants of the words I spoke to you.

Dwindling embers of the fire I had with you.

Abyss

This space between the memory and the moments with you is a void with no end.

Avalon Breen

Predestined

If time could tell our fate,

Would he have warned me of you?

I can't help feeling I'm entrapped in destiny's stalemate

Avalon Breen

What it's worth

I gave you poems when you only gave me words.

I gave you gazes when you only gave me glimpses.

I gave you mouthfuls when you only gave me a taste.

I gave you stars when you only gave me darkness.

And I gave you love when you only ever gave me...

Heartbreak.

Avalon Breen

Symphonies

Our eyes play symphonies of words unspoken

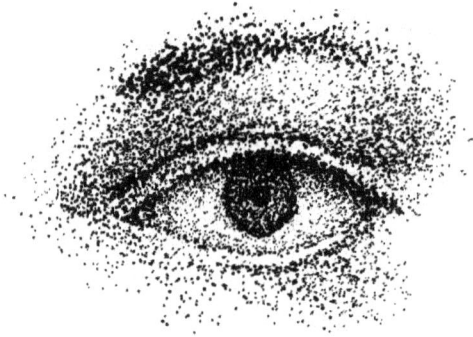

Ultimate Weakness

I feel pain in parts of me I never knew existed.

Looking back, I wish my heart could have just resisted.

Avalon Breen

Pleasure/Pain

That heavenly sigh is now buried under the memory of a hellish goodbye.

Avalon Breen

Fragile Material

I had those handle-with-care eyes,

Something you never even realised.

Perhaps you were too busy with the look of my thighs

Or maybe too fixated on perfecting those lies.

I must admit, it was an impenetrable disguise,

One where you were deaf to the sound

A heart makes when it cries and

Even the collapse of a love when it dies.

Avalon Breen

Existence of Meaning

I'm trying to find the meaning in what we had.

The greater plan.

The lesson.

Sifting through the empty eternities and hollow soliloquies,

Trying to see if it all really was a blessing.

But if my retrospect is correct then

Reflecting back the only thing I see,

Is that broken hearts were our destiny.

The Difference

My heart was fragile while your hands were fickle.

Avalon Breen

Entrapment

I'm a prisoner to the memory of you,

Despite my attempts at trying to create something new,

I'm still haunted by the soft moments of gazing at your skin,

Overwhelmed by the impossible task of trying to take you all in.

Those eyes reflecting back the warmth of the sunlight,

I swear I'd never see the universe gleam so blindingly bright,

Once hopeful of the legacy our love would leave,

Now it's only something that my heart grieves.

Avalon Breen

What We're Afraid Of

There are things in this life that are much more terrifying than
monsters.

Like fingerprints that can't be washed away,

Smiles that stain eyes and laughter that makes angels sigh,

Memories that can't be erased because it's impossible to forget
an unforgettable face.

Realisation

The thing that haunts me the most

Is that it doesn't haunt you at all.

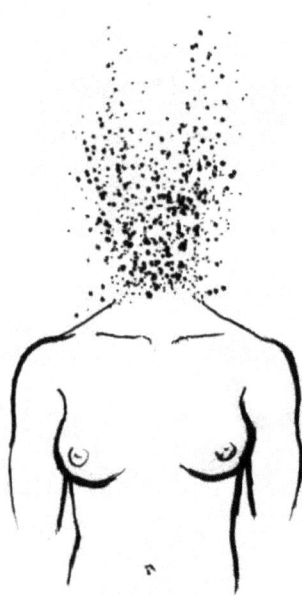

Avalon Breen

Shakespeare

I coloured in your words with the sounds I wish I heard.

I would white-out your mistakes

While I pressed backspace on all the heartache

All the transgressions I had to erase…

I put an upper-case on all the good times and lower-case on all
the bad nights

Can you think of a better playwright?

I made them all believe this tragedy was a fantasy

In the end I fooled even me.

Avalon Breen

The Price of Pride

Our love evaporated in the heat of our egos.

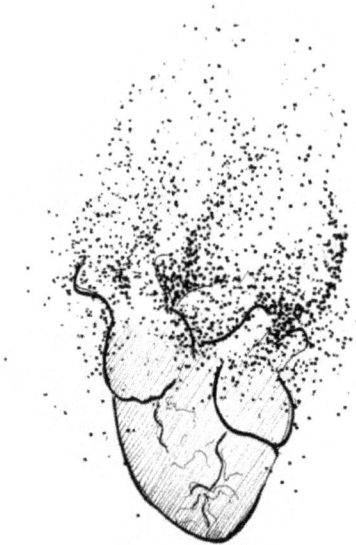

Avalon Breen

Love > Lust

From the vantage point of now, I can see where our inevitable

demise began.

We spoke of fondness but never of giving,

We spoke of affection but never of devotion.

We spoke of attention but never of forgiving,

We sang songs of love and adoration,

Pretending we were each other's salvation.

I can't think of an emptier demonstration.

It was nothing more than a prolonged flirtation.

A relationship like that can only ever end in fragmentation.

Avalon Breen

Double Meaning

Before you, oblivion used to just be a word.

Now it's the memory of what we shared.

Soaked in Sorrow

My heart is saturated in your empty promises.

Modified

I'm losing hope in the face of trying to reprogram myself after you

Because you're a virus that's infiltrated too deep.

I failed the first time at letting you take over completely.

It won't be long before I crash again…

Avalon Breen

Walking Contradiction

No wonder we didn't work.

You sought aesthetics and I sought authenticity.

You sought quantity and I sought depth.

You sought superficial and I sought spiritual.

You sought lust and I sought love.

Endless

I'm still drowning in thoughts of you

Avalon Breen

Fatal

The thought of you intoxicates me,

The touch of you paralyses me,

The warmth of you burns me,

The look of you dismantles me;

Oh, how the love of you kills me

Avalon Breen

The Puppet Master

My heart no longer beats

To the tempo of your ego.

It will not rise and fall

To the sound of your voice

Anymore.

Because finally, I realise

That your love was nothing

More than a placebo.

Suffocation

Loving you made me realise my addiction to asphyxia.

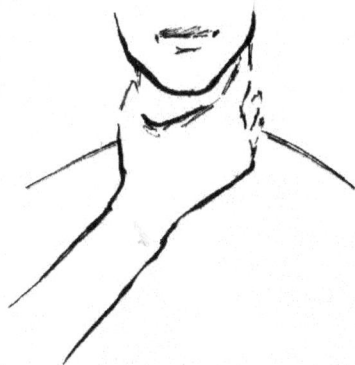

Avalon Breen

Ambivalence Breeds Regret

You may not have ever been mine,

We passed each other too many times,

Letting words sit in the bottom of our throats,

Always swallowing them back with the

Bitter taste etched on our palates.

We became cowards in the face of feelings,

Waiting. Wanting the other to take that plunge,

To dive into the depths of a desperate dream.

But you didn't.

I didn't.

We didn't.

Unfillable

How I wish that your love had not carved holes so deep into me
that not a single person since has managed to fill.

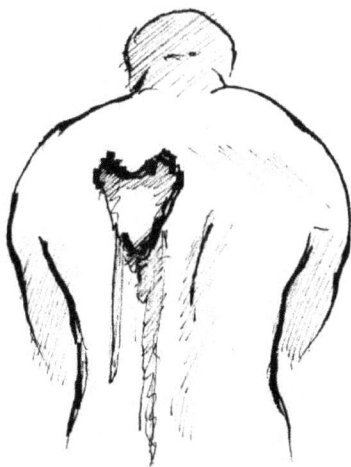

Avalon Breen

Lost in translation

Meanings are subjective, you cannot tell me they aren't.

Like how my forever meant eternity

And yours meant temporarily.

Avalon Breen

Sadist

Writing about you is like reopening a wound. One I used to believe I had healed.

Then I realise that these scars are just another gateway; to all the ghosts that still haunt this body.

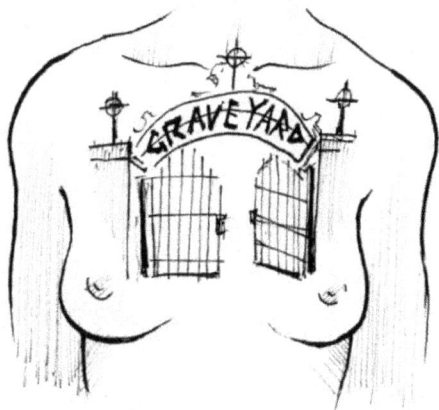

Avalon Breen

Invisible Load

Your voice spoke to me in a language that was too loud for
words and too heavy for sounds

Yet my heart still carries the weight of it.

Avalon Breen

Chasm

There is no greater distance than that of two people,

Side by side

And out of love

Hopeless

They ask me how to spell love and I keep writing your name.

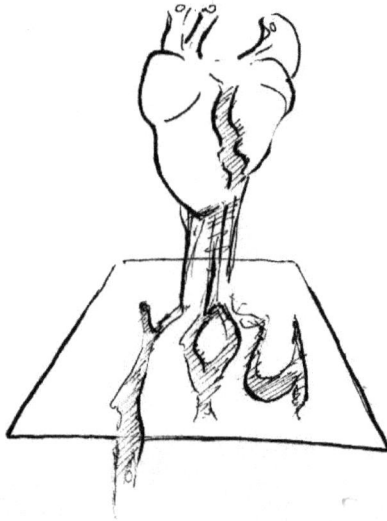

Avalon Breen

Avoidance

Sometimes I wonder if we only used "I love you" to colour in the silence.

Avalon Breen

Self-Destructive

You burn

I bleed

So tell me

Why won't these

Hearts ever concede?

Avalon Breen

Oblivious

They say that silence is golden

That's because they don't know

It's my words you have stolen

And my voice you have broken

Avalon Breen

Toxic

Poison is a label with misleading symbols.

You coloured its syllables with silk

And made my decision

To drink from

You simple.

Avalon Breen

Shared Guilt

We have blood on our hands

From the hearts we break

And the lies we fake

Avalon Breen

See-through

I?

I was always looking right at you.

And you?

You were always looking right through me.

Avalon Breen

Spelling Errors

I spell regret:

Y O U

Avalon Breen

He loves me, He loves me not....

So pick my soul to pieces like petals off a flower

This heart you've long since devoured.

102

Avalon Breen

Wholeness

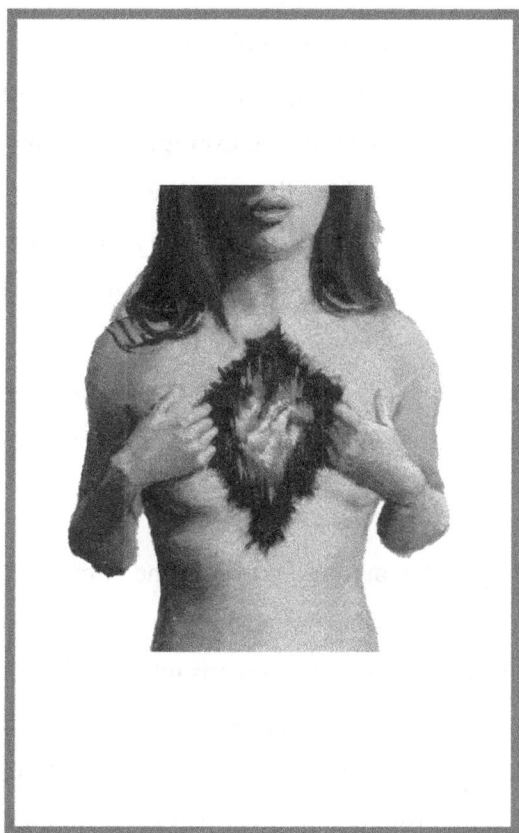

Avalon Breen

Wholeness can be defined as a state of completeness that is harmonious and unified. It is the opposite of brokenness. When we think of being whole, we imagine a state that no longer yearns for other pieces to be attained, because we realise that we are the sum of all the parts we need to feel fulfilled and content.

Yet many believe they are incomplete and that finding their lover will make them whole again. This belief is rooted in many old idea; one greatly romanticised example of this can be found in Plato's Symposium, where the poet Aristophanes gives his account of incomplete love by drawing on a myth that claims humans were originally two beings combined as one. They had four limbs, two faces, and were twice the size they are now. Males were said to be descended from the sun, females from the earth, and the androgynous from the moon, because the moon is a combination of both the earth and the sun.

The god's feared the immense power of the humans and turned to Zeus to deal with them. Not wishing to destroy the human race, Zeus decided to split the humans into two, but this became a curse that left the humans longing for their other half. In the beginning, many died, while others continued to desperately throw their arms around their other half in an attempt to form one being again. They no longer ate, they became inactive, and all they could focus on was their desire to return to their original state as one whole being.

It is a beautiful and captivating myth, one which describes well the innate and intense longing humans have to find their "other half.". Stories like this however, perpetuate the idea that we are imperfect and incomplete when alone. This leaves us desperately trying to fill a void that is simply a perversion of our true nature. When, in fact, we are already whole – perfect, just as we are.

To truly love another, we must love out of a place that is much deeper than just a longing to satisfy or satiate our loneliness. If we approach love from this perspective, our partner will always fall short. We will place unrealistic expectations on them to fulfil us, when it is in fact up to us to ultimately find fulfilment within ourselves. When we come together as two complete beings, we engage in something that is much more beautiful and profound than a perceived need to complete each other.

In essence, there is no journey towards or back to wholeness; rather, the journey is the process of remembering you are already whole. This is what the final section of the book is about: reclaiming the power you have as an individual – a complete person - and remembering that only you can find fulfilment and happiness within yourself.

You'll notice that the style of writing is noticeably different in the latter half of the book as the focus shifts to one of personal healing and individual awakening. I have made the final half much shorter than the first as I plan to produce an entirely separate book that pertains to healing and fulfilment. The central message, however, remains the same: happiness and wholeness cannot be procured, bought, or found, because you have it within you already.

In this final section of the book, you'll find a pathway back to who you truly are.

Ocean Depth

I was once slowly immersed within the sea of you. Now, I'm gradually adapting to land again

And soon, I'll be completely dry of all your droplets.

The Revival

I'm using the ash of our love as the soil to plant seeds of fresh beginnings and golden blessings.

Always Worthy

I am not without flaw, that's for sure,

But I will not be made to feel guilty for deserving more.

You see, this heart was made for love, not war, and destruction
was all you ever intended it for.

Avalon Breen

Growth

I used to burn for you

Then I bled from you

Now I bloom without you

Avalon Breen

You Decide

Attachment is a leech

That survives on the blood of possession.

I tried to kill the leech with my sweetness

Till I remembered the salt I held within me.

The Distraction

I blamed you for being another victim of my relentless saviour-complex. I saw you being swallowed by a force invisible to most, and my selfish desire to stop what was destined to break consumed me. And so I plunged head-first into the depths of your darkness, when I was yet to find the light within my own.

Put Yourself First

Looking back, I can't even begin to count the "I love you's" I so generously entrusted you with.

Just how I can't even count the myriad of "I love you's" I should have said to myself instead.

Guilt Stunts Spiritual Progression

I remember suffocating myself in guilt. A self-imposed prison with a life sentence. Guilt is a quicksand where, the more we feed our sense of shame, the faster we sink. Recognise your humanness and do not fall into the trap of thinking you require redemption for living your life as best you can. Only you can liberate yourself from your cage.

There Is No Alternative

I tried to substitute having for being. I believed that having love was being love. But I went about it all backwards. I finally understand that to truly have anything, we must first become what it is we seek, before we can ever hope of meaningfully acquiring anything.

Avalon Breen

Un-conditioning

I need to remind myself that the bleeding is not always beautiful.

The Nature of Forgiving

Forgiveness is soft

That is why whenever I think of you

I pray you are well

The Quiet Moments

Healing is not always dramatic and loud. It is often silent, taking place in the tender moments spent with yourself. In the sun-streaked afternoon when you dance in the light or play soft music while infused with the scented aroma of candles. Healing is the process of connecting with yourself again.

Avalon Breen

Relinquish

If you wish to heal,

Sink into surrender.

Avalon Breen

Caution

I was caught up in the noise, the fireworks, and the endless theatrics of it all. I was prey to pretty words, forgetting that the deadliest of poisons are always administered by the most beautiful of people.

Avalon Breen

Reminder

To Remember:

Control is not synonymous with courage

Art

Poetry is the process of being present with the pain.

Moving Forward

I walked away

Because I realised the price it cost to stay

With a heart that only ever knows how to stray

Avalon Breen

No Shortcuts

The only way to dissolve heartache is to feel it.

Avalon Breen

Ready is a Relative Term

Bravery requires the presence of the unknown;

Therefore, waiting is the slow death of courage.

Avalon Breen

Water Purifies

The same tears

I once used

To drown my

Bones in sorrow

Are now the

Water I feed

To my soul

As I watch

Us both grow.

Avalon Breen

Experience Provides Meaning

Pain taught me presence,

Oppression taught me openness

And heartache taught me healing.

Poisoned Snake

Holding onto a toxic relationship is like grasping onto a snake
that has coiled around you.

The more you struggle against it, the more the pain just deepens.

If you truly wish for the pain to end, let go.

Avalon Breen

Patience in Persistence

I'm still learning how to weave the darker parts of me into
tender works of art.

Cleansing

Tears are the elixir of release.

Discovering Strength

You have the ability to break

And you also have the ability to unite.

Avalon Breen

Room for Recovery

Give yourself space and time when mending your soul;

Expectations are just more weight to carry.

It Starts With You

Love, if not given to yourself first, will always be conditional when given to others.

Awareness

Self-love is actualised through the wholehearted acceptance that you are not perfect and you will never be. By realising your journey here is one of growth not flawlessness.

Avalon Breen

Make Your Heart Grateful

Pain is transformed into strength when there is no fear of its presence, only thankfulness.

Avalon Breen

Easy is Never Worthwhile

Self-love does not always seem loving

It means work

It takes effort

You have to commit

Practice

Patience

Persistence

It's the new awareness that you are worth all the energy and
focus it takes to ensure you live your highest truth.

Avalon Breen

Incompatible

Control and love cannot reside in the same place.

Avalon Breen

Recognition

When we try to use an external source as a means of fulfilment,
we must become aware of the absence of love within ourselves.

(The void)

Avalon Breen

Reclaiming Power

I selflessly gave you my days and, as they turned into years, I
never realised the value of time.

Starting now, I reclaim these days as they were always mine.

Avalon Breen

Set Ablaze

If I have the ability to burn like fire, I also have the ability to rise like smoke, forever higher.

Progression is Never Passive

Just reading beautiful words is not enough in the process of mending our souls. We must actively release our pain, our hurt, and our sorrow. For it will become a dead weight with a heaviness that diminishes our hearts levity.

A Far Worse Fate

It is a far greater tragedy to have a heart that is closed than one that is broken.

Understanding

I'm still learning the art of letting go, so forgive me on the days
when I am flattened under the weight of woe.

Avalon Breen

Finally I See

I realise now that the way you loved me was the way I loved myself.

(I didn't)

Avalon Breen

A Bountiful Cup

Your capacity for growth is the capacity for your giving.

Avalon Breen

The Truth about Healing

We must not confuse healing with romanticisation of our wounds. Too often, we proclaim being cured and moving past our hurts when really, we are moving back into them. Healing is release not restraint. Whether you carry your wounds around with you as a badge or a burden, the weight is still the same.

Avalon Breen

Perspective

I used to believe this life was poison and you were my cure.

Until I recognised you were the poison and this life is the cure.

Avalon Breen

Beauty in Imperfection

You should be scared of loving again;

It reminds you you're still human.

Pain can be Powerful

Don't use your wounds as your weapons for manipulation.

Avalon Breen

Imperceptible

You mustn't be fooled just because your pain is palpable and your healing is hidden.

The process of being healed can often be invisible to the eye but never to the knowing of the soul.

Passion above Everything

You're not here for perfect

You're here for purpose.

Deep Healing

Too often, we fall into the trap of believing our healing is finished. We think that once we have healed something, we have finally made it to the Promised Land, and that our journey ceases. This is never the case. It is a continual process, one that you have been engaging in for lifetimes.

Avalon Breen

Avalon Breen